CANINE CUISINE

First published by Parragon Books Ltd 2014

Parragon
Chartist House
15-17 Trim Street
Bath BA1 1HA, UK
www.parragon.com

Copyright © Parragon Books Ltd 2014
Produced by Tall Tree Ltd
Photography by Michael Wicks
Illustrations by the Apple Art Agency

ISBN 978-1-4723-3725-2

Printed in China

CANINE CUISINE

Tasty treats for your four-legged friend

Shawn Sherry

PaRRagon

Bath · New York · Singapore · Hong Kong · Cologne · Delhi
Melbourne · Amsterdam · Johannesburg · Shenzhen

Contents

1

6 Introduction

2

Tail-waggin' meat-lovers' recipes

10-11 Cheeseburger chow

12-13 Poultry perfection

14-15 Picnic treats

16-17 One fish, chew fish

18-19 Bacon bone-anza

Two-paws-up veggie recipes

22-23 Pooch salad

24-25 Healthy rewards

26-27 Paw-pkin pie

28-29 Bow-wow veggie delight

Howl-iday fun recipes

32-33 Canine carrot Easter biscuits

34-35 Turkey dinner

36-37 Honey heart biscuits

38-39 Scary sweet potato crunch

40-41 Birthday parties

42-43 Birthday pup-cakes

44-45 Blueberry birthday cake

Gourmet desserts

48-49 Peanut butter pooch bites

50-51 Carob peanut-butter pups

52-53 Sweet treats

54-55 Blueberry biscuits

Allergen-free recipes

58-59 Sweet potato crisps

60-61 Pear and banana biscuits

62-63 Duck delight

64 Index

Home cooking is the perfect way to keep an eye on what your dog eats and to make sure they have a healthy and nutritious diet. Whether you're a master chef or just a pet lover, this cookbook will show you how to make delicious meals and treats that your dog will love.

Sourcing ingredients

Most of the ingredients used in the recipes in this book can be bought from high-street food shops and supermarkets. A few, such as carob chips and dried apple pieces, can be sourced from health-food shops and online food suppliers.

How much food?

This depends on your dog's size and lifestyle. Some recipes will make one meal for a large dog but up to four for a smaller one. Some recipes are entire meals, but others are for treats or snacks, which should be eaten in small amounts, in addition to regular meals.

Storage

To make sure that your home-cooked food lasts longer, keep it in an airtight plastic container or a ziplock bag before putting it into the refrigerator or freezer. Storage times can be found at the end of each recipe.

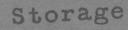

Food allergies

You may discover that your pet pooch finds it hard to stomach certain foods, such as those containing wheat. The final section of this book contains a few allergen-free recipes to satisfy the most sensitive of stomachs. If you are uncertain how your dog will tolerate any of the ingredients, then please consult your vet.

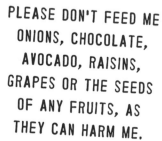

PLEASE DON'T FEED ME ONIONS, CHOCOLATE, AVOCADO, RAISINS, GRAPES OR THE SEEDS OF ANY FRUITS, AS THEY CAN HARM ME.

CHAPTER 1

Tail-waggin' meat-lovers' recipes

CHEESEBURGER CHOW

1 Preheat the oven to 190°C/375°F/Gas Mark 5.

2 Pour the oats and stock into the bowl and mix together until thoroughly combined.

3 Slowly add the Parmesan cheese to the oat mixture and mix well to combine.

4 Put the oat mixture on to a clean surface and roll it out until it is about 1 cm/⅜ inch thick.

5 Cut out as many shapes as you can, depending on the size of your cutter, and place them on the baking sheet. Bake for approximately 30 minutes.

6 Let the shapes cool before serving any to your pup.

7 The shapes can be kept in the refrigerator for up to two weeks.

POULTRY PERFECTION

EQUIPMENT

OVEN
BAKING TRAY
MEASURING JUG
TWO SAUCEPANS
SCALES
VEGETABLE PEELER
CHOPPING BOARD
KNIFE
LARGE MIXING BOWL
MIXING SPOON

1 Preheat the oven to 180°C/350°F/Gas Mark 4. Place the chicken in the baking tray and cook it for about 30 minutes, or until the chicken is cooked throughout and the meat is no longer pink.

2 Heat 350 ml/12 fl oz of the water in a saucepan and, once boiling, pour in the rice. Let the rice cook on a low heat for 45 minutes or until the water is fully absorbed.

3 Peel the carrot, then chop the carrot and green beans into small cubes and add the peas. Put the vegetables and the remaining water into the other saucepan and boil them for 5 minutes.

4 Place the cooked chicken on to the chopping board and cut it into small cubes.

5 Put the chicken, rice and vegetables into the bowl and mix together until thoroughly combined.

6 Allow the mixture to cool to room temperature before serving to your pup.

7 This will make 1–4 servings, depending on the size of your dog. It can be kept in the refrigerator for two days, or frozen for up to one month.

INGREDIENTS

1 LARGE, BONELESS CHICKEN BREAST, ABOUT 225 G/8 OZ

575 ML/18 FL OZ WATER

150 G/5½ OZ RICE

100 G/3½ OZ CARROT

100 G/3½ OZ GREEN BEANS

100 G/3½ OZ PEAS

12

YUM!

STRAWBERRY PUP-SICLES

1 Cut 115 g/4 oz of strawberries into quarters, slicing off the stems, and put them into a blender.

2 Pour 125 ml/4 fl oz of water into a blender and blend the ingredients until they form a smooth mixture.

3 Pour the strawberry mixture into a 6-10 compartment ice-cube tray and put it in a freezer until frozen. These are great to bring along to a picnic to help your pup keep cool in the heat.

PERFECT MANNERS

Picnic treats

Alfresco dining is absolutely paw-fect!

READY FOR THE PICNIC

TAIL MIX

1 Preheat the oven to 150°C/300°F/Gas Mark 2. Cut an apple, a pear, a banana and a carrot into thin slices. Place the slices on to a baking sheet.

2 Bake them in the oven for 30 minutes.

3 Turn the slices over and bake them for an additional 30 minutes or until the slices feel dry.

4 Let the slices cool before serving any to your pup. The slices can be kept in the refrigerator for a week.

ONE FISH, CHEW FISH

EQUIPMENT

OVEN
SCALES
MEASURING JUG
LARGE MIXING BOWL
MIXING SPOON
ROLLING PIN
SHAPED CUTTER
BAKING SHEET

1 Preheat the oven to 190°C/375°F/Gas Mark 5.

2 Pour the oats and stock into the bowl and mix together until thoroughly combined.

3 Slowly add the Parmesan cheese to the oat mixture and mix well to combine.

4 Put the oat mixture on to a clean surface and roll it out until it is about 1 cm/½ inch thick.

5 Cut out as many shapes as you can, depending on the size of your cutter, and place them on the baking sheet. Bake for approximately 30 minutes.

6 Let the shapes cool before serving any to your pup.

7 The shapes can be kept in the refrigerator for up to two weeks.

INGREDIENTS

450 g/1 lb ROLLED OATS

225 ml/8 fl oz FISH STOCK

60 g/2¼ oz GRATED
PARMESAN CHEESE

BACON BONE-ANZA

1 Preheat the oven to 190°C/375°F/Gas Mark 5.

2 Cook the bacon in the frying pan for 10 minutes or until it is crispy.

3 Allow the bacon to drain on kitchen paper, before putting it on to the chopping board and cutting it into small pieces.

4 Put the rolled oats, bacon and honey into the bowl and mix together until thoroughly combined.

5 Place 12 cupcake cases into the tin and scoop the mixture into the cases, filling each one to the top.

6 Bake in the oven for approximately 20 minutes, or until the tops are crunchy.

7 Let the cupcakes cool before serving any to your pup.

8 The cupcakes can be kept in the refrigerator for up to four days.

INGREDIENTS

2 RASHERS OF STREAKY BACON

450 G/1 LB ROLLED OATS

60 ML/2 FL OZ HONEY

CHAPTER 2

Two-paws-up veggie recipes

POOCH SALAD

EQUIPMENT

SCALES
VEGETABLE PEELER
CHOPPING BOARD
KNIFE
LARGE MIXING BOWL
MIXING SPOON
MEASURING JUG

1 Wash the lettuce and peel the cucumber, carrot and sweet potato.

2 Cut the cucumber, carrot and sweet potato into cubes, measuring approximately 1 cm/½ inch across, and put them into the bowl.

3 Chop the lettuce into small pieces and add these to the bowl.

4 Pour the yogurt into the bowl and stir the ingredients until everything has been coated thoroughly. Feed the salad to your pup immediately.

5 This will make 1–4 servings, depending on the size of your dog. It can be kept in the refrigerator for two days.

INGREDIENTS

200 g/7 oz LETTUCE

100 g/3½ oz CUCUMBER

150 g/5½ oz CARROT

150 g/5½ oz SWEET POTATO

60 ml/2 fl oz LOW-FAT YOGURT

Healthy rewards

Tasty treats to keep your pup in tip-top condition.

GO FETCH CELERY STICKS

1 Cut the leaves off the top of three celery sticks and cut each stick into pieces about 10 cm/4 inches long.

2 Spread peanut butter into the inner channel of each celery stick.

3 Serve as a healthy snack.

FRUIT PUPS

1 Core an apple, then cut the apple, a banana and 60 g/2¼ oz of strawberries into small cubes.

2 Place the fruit cubes into a bowl and mix with 60 g/ 2¼ oz of blueberries. Serve the fruit pup to your dog.

TIP

Boil the fruit in some water for 5 minutes to soften it a little if your pup likes their food to be a little less crunchy.

PAW-PKIN PIE

EQUIPMENT

OVEN
SCALES
MEASURING JUG
LARGE MIXING BOWL
MIXING SPOON
ROLLING PIN
KNIFE OR LARGE
ROUND CUTTER
12-HOLE CUPCAKE TIN

1. Preheat the oven to 190°C/375°F/Gas Mark 5.

2. Put the flour, water and 150 ml/5 fl oz of pumpkin purée into the mixing bowl.

3. Mix the ingredients together thoroughly to form a dough. Place the dough on to a clean surface and roll out until it is about 0.5 cm/¼ inch thick.

4. Cut the dough into 12 circles, measuring about 15 cm/6 inches across, using the knife or the cutter.

5. Place the circles into the wells of the cupcake tin, making sure that some excess dough sits above each cupcake well.

6. Put a spoonful of the remaining pumpkin purée into each well. Then take the excess dough around the edges of each cupcake well and pinch each pie closed to form a parcel.

7. Bake the pies for 30 minutes, or until the top of each pie has browned slightly.

8. Let the pies cool before serving any to your pup.

9. The pies can be kept in the refrigerator for up to four days.

INGREDIENTS

450 g/1 lb PLAIN FLOUR

125 ml/4 fl oz WATER

350 ml/12 fl oz PUMPKIN PURÉE

26

BOW-WOW VEGGIE DELIGHT

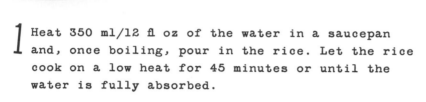

1 Heat 350 ml/12 fl oz of the water in a saucepan and, once boiling, pour in the rice. Let the rice cook on a low heat for 45 minutes or until the water is fully absorbed.

2 Peel the carrot, then chop the carrot, green beans and squash into small cubes and add the peas. Put the vegetables and the remaining water into the other saucepan and boil them for 5 minutes.

3 Chop the cucumber into small cubes.

4 Pour the rice, carrots, green beans, squash, peas and cucumber into the bowl and mix them together thoroughly.

5 Allow the mixture to cool to room temperature before serving to your pup.

6 This will make 1–4 servings, depending on the size of your dog. It can be kept in the refrigerator for two days, or frozen for up to one month.

INGREDIENTS

575 ml/18 fl oz WATER

150 g/5½ oz RICE

100 g/3½ oz CARROT

100 g/3½ oz GREEN BEANS

100 g/3½ oz BUTTERNUT SQUASH

100 g/3½ oz PEAS

100 g/3½ oz CUCUMBER

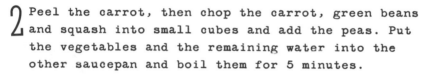

CHAPTER 3

Howl-iday
fun recipes

CANINE CARROT EASTER BISCUITS

1 Preheat the oven to 190°C/375°F/Gas Mark 5.

2 Peel the carrot and cut it into small pieces. Put the pieces into the blender and add the water.

3 Blend the ingredients thoroughly until they form a smooth mixture.

4 Pour the oats and carrot mixture into the bowl and mix them together thoroughly.

5 Place the oat mixture on to a clean surface and roll it out until it is about 1 cm/½ inch thick.

6 Cut out as many Easter shapes as you can, depending on the size of your cutter, and place them on the baking sheet.

7 Bake the biscuits for 30 minutes, or until they are hard, then leave them to cool before serving any to your pup.

8 The biscuits can be kept in the refrigerator for up to two weeks.

EQUIPMENT

OVEN
SCALES
VEGETABLE PEELER
CHOPPING BOARD
KNIFE
BLENDER
MEASURING JUG
LARGE MIXING BOWL
MIXING SPOON
ROLLING PIN
EASTER SHAPED CUTTER
BAKING SHEET

INGREDIENTS

225 G/8 OZ CARROT

225 ML/8 FL OZ WATER

450 G/1 LB ROLLED OATS

TURKEY DINNER

1 Preheat the oven to 180°C/350°F/Gas Mark 4. Place the turkey in the baking tray and cook it for about 30 minutes, or until the turkey is cooked throughout and the meat is no longer pink.

2 Heat 350 ml/12 fl oz of the water in a saucepan and, once boiling, pour in the rice. Let the rice cook on a low heat for 45 minutes or until the water is fully absorbed.

3 Peel the carrot, then chop the carrot and green beans into small cubes and add the peas. Put the vegetables and the remaining water into the other saucepan and boil them for 5 minutes.

4 Place the cooked turkey on to the chopping board and cut it into small cubes.

5 Put the turkey, rice, vegetables and cranberries into the bowl and mix together until thoroughly combined.

6 Allow the mixture to cool to room temperature before serving to your pup.

7 This will make 1–4 servings, depending on the size of your dog. It can be kept in the refrigerator for two days, or frozen for up to one month.

WOOF

EQUIPMENT

OVEN
SCALES
BAKING TRAY
MEASURING JUG
TWO SAUCEPANS
VEGETABLE PEELER
CHOPPING BOARD
KNIFE
LARGE MIXING BOWL
MIXING SPOON

INGREDIENTS

1 LARGE, BONELESS TURKEY BREAST, ABOUT 225 G/8 OZ

575 ML/18 FL OZ WATER

150 G/5½ OZ RICE

100 G/3½ OZ CARROT

100 G/3½ OZ GREEN BEANS

100 G/3½ OZ PEAS

100 G/3½ OZ DRIED CRANBERRIES

HONEY HEART BISCUITS

EQUIPMENT

OVEN
SCALES
MEASURING JUG
LARGE MIXING BOWL
MIXING SPOON
ROLLING PIN
HEART-SHAPED CUTTERS
BAKING SHEET

1 Preheat the oven to 190°C/375°F/Gas Mark 5.

2 Pour the rolled oats, honey and water into the bowl and mix together until thoroughly combined.

3 Put the oat mixture on to a clean surface and roll it out until it is about 1 cm/½ inch thick.

4 Cut out as many biscuits as you can, depending on the size of your cutter, and place them on the baking sheet. Bake for approximately 30 minutes.

5 Let the biscuits cool before serving any to your pup.

6 The biscuits can be kept in the refrigerator for up to two weeks.

INGREDIENTS

450 G/1 LB ROLLED OATS

115 G/4 OZ HONEY

225 ML/8 FL OZ WATER

SCARY SWEET
POTATO CRUNCH

1 Preheat the oven to 190°C/375°F/Gas Mark 5.

2 Peel the sweet potato and cut it into small pieces.
Put the pieces into the blender and add the water. Blend
the ingredients together until they form a smooth mixture.

3 Pour the oats and the sweet potato mixture into the bowl and mix
them together thoroughly.

4 Place the oat mixture on to a clean surface and roll it out
until it is about 1 cm/½ inch thick.

5 Cut out as many Halloween shapes as you can, depending on
the size of your cutters, and place them on the baking
sheet. Bake for approximately 30 minutes, or until they
are hard.

6 Let the shapes cool before serving any to your pup.
Once cool, you can make small holes and decorate the
biscuits with the dried cranberries.

7 The shapes can be kept in the refrigerator for up to
two weeks.

EQUIPMENT

OVEN
SCALES
VEGETABLE PEELER
CHOPPING BOARD
KNIFE
BLENDER
MEASURING JUG
LARGE MIXING BOWL
MIXING SPOON
ROLLING PIN
HALLOWEEN SHAPED
CUTTERS
BAKING SHEET

INGREDIENTS

225 G/8 OZ SWEET POTATO

225 ML/8 FL OZ WATER

450 G/1 LB ROLLED
OATS

DRIED CRANBERRIES
FOR DECORATION

Birthday parties

Helpful hints for the perfect pooch party.

PARTY TIME!

CAROB-COVERED PAWBERRIES

1 Place 115 g/4 oz of carob chips into a microwaveable cup and pour 30 ml/1 fl oz of rapeseed oil over the top.

2 Put the cup into a microwave and heat on full power for 1 minute, or until the carob has melted.

3 Dip strawberries into the melted carob, so that they are half covered, and place them on a sheet of greaseproof paper.

4 Put the strawberries in a refrigerator and serve once the carob has hardened.

BIRTHDAY BREAKFAST PUPMEAL

1 Core an apple and cut it into small cubes.

2 Pour 225 ml/8 fl oz of water into a ceramic bowl and put it in a microwave on full power for 2 minutes.

3 Take the warm water from the microwave and pour it on top of 225 g/8 oz of rolled oats.

4 Stir the ingredients until the water has been absorbed into the oats.

5 Mix the chopped apple and 60 g/2¼ oz of fresh blueberries into the oatmeal. Let the mixture cool and then serve.

WHAT'S THAT IN DOG YEARS?

BIRTHDAY PUP-CAKES

EQUIPMENT

OVEN
SCALES
BLENDER
MEASURING JUG
LARGE MIXING BOWL
MIXING SPOON
12 CUPCAKE CASES
12-HOLE CUPCAKE TIN
KITCHEN SPOON

1 Preheat the oven to 190°C/375°F/Gas Mark 5.

2 Wash the cherries and put 100 g/3½ oz of them into the blender and add the water.

3 Blend the ingredients together until they form a smooth mixture.

4 Pour the oats and the cherry mixture into the bowl and mix them together thoroughly.

5 Place 12 cupcake cases into the cupcake tin. Scoop the oat and cherry mixture into the cases, filling them to the top.

6 Place a half cherry on top of each cupcake.

7 Bake the cupcakes for approximately 20 minutes, or until the tops are crunchy.

8 Let the cupcakes cool before serving any to your pup.

9 The cupcakes can be kept in the refrigerator for up to four days.

INGREDIENTS

150 G/5¼ OZ PITTED CHERRIES

225 ML/8 FL OZ WATER

450 G/1 LB ROLLED OATS

42

BLUEBERRY BIRTHDAY CAKE

1 Preheat the oven to 190°C/375°F/Gas Mark 5.

2 Wash the blueberries and put them into the blender with the peeled banana and the water. Blend the ingredients thoroughly until they form a smooth mixture.

3 Pour the oats and the blueberry mixture into the bowl and mix them together thoroughly.

4 Use your hands to roll the mixture to create one large ball and three smaller ones.

5 Place the larger ball on to the baking sheet, pushing down to flatten it slightly.

6 Place the smaller balls on to the baking sheet around the top of the larger ball, to create a paw-print shape. Again, push down to flatten the smaller balls a little.

7 Bake the cake for 30 minutes, or until the top of the cake is slightly crunchy.

8 Let the cake cool before serving any slices to your pup.

9 The cake can be kept in the refrigerator for up to four days.

EQUIPMENT

OVEN
SCALES
BLENDER
MEASURING JUG
LARGE MIXING BOWL
MIXING SPOON
BAKING SHEET

INGREDIENTS

200 G/7 OZ BLUEBERRIES

1 BANANA

225 ML/8 FL OZ WATER

450 G/1 LB ROLLED OATS

CHAPTER 4

Gourmet desserts

PEANUT-BUTTER POOCH BITES

EQUIPMENT

OVEN
SCALES
MEASURING JUG
LARGE MIXING BOWL
MIXING SPOON
BROWNIE TIN
SPATULA
LARGE MICROWAVEABLE CUP
MICROWAVE

1 Preheat the oven to 190°C/375°F/Gas Mark 5.

2 Put the rolled oats, peanut butter and water into the bowl and mix them together thoroughly.

3 Scoop the mixture into the brownie tin and smooth the surface using the spatula.

4 Bake for 30 minutes, or until the top is slightly crunchy, and leave it to cool.

5 Put the carob chips into the large cup and pour the rapeseed oil on top.

6 Heat in the microwave at full power for 1 minute 20 seconds. Take the cup out of the microwave and mix the melted carob and oil until they are thoroughly combined.

7 Pour the carob mixture over the top of the peanut-butter bars and use the spatula to smooth the surface.

8 Put the brownie tin in the refrigerator to harden the carob. Cut the mixture into small bars before serving any to your pup.

9 The bars can be kept in the refrigerator for four days, or in the freezer for one month.

INGREDIENTS

450 G/1 LB ROLLED OATS

150 G/5½ OZ PEANUT BUTTER

225 ML/8 FL OZ WATER

150 G/5½ OZ CAROB CHIPS

60 ML/2 FL OZ RAPESEED OIL

CAROB PEANUT-BUTTER PUPS

EQUIPMENT
SCALES
LARGE MICROWAVEABLE CUP
MEASURING JUG
MICROWAVE
MIXING SPOON
12 CUPCAKE CASES
12-HOLE CUPCAKE TIN
KITCHEN SPOONS

1 Put the carob chips into the large cup and pour the rapeseed oil on top.

2 Heat in the microwave at full power for 1 minute 20 seconds. Take the cup out of the microwave and mix the melted carob and oil until they are thoroughly combined.

3 Place 12 cupcake cases into the cupcake tin. Put a spoonful of melted carob into the cupcake cases and smoothe the inside of each to create a hollow carob shell.

4 Put the cupcake tin in the refrigerator for 2 hours, or until the carob is hard.

5 Put a spoonful of peanut butter into each carob shell and press down, so that it does not stick out above the top of the cupcake case.

6 Pour the remaining melted carob on top of each cupcake so that the peanut butter is covered.

7 Put the cupcake tin back into the refrigerator to harden the carob before serving any to your pup.

8 The cupcakes can be kept in the refrigerator for four days, or in the freezer for up to a month.

INGREDIENTS
150 G/5½ OZ CAROB CHIPS
60 ML/2 FL OZ RAPESEED OIL
150 G/5½ OZ PEANUT BUTTER

Sweet treats

Try these simple treats on your favourite hound.

FROZEN BANANA TREATS

1 Mash two bananas and put them into a bowl with 60 g/2¼ oz of peanut butter and 500 ml/17 fl oz of low-fat vanilla yogurt.

2 Mix the ingredients until they are thoroughly combined.

3 Pour the mixture into a 24 compartment ice-cube tray and put it in a freezer. Wait until the treats have frozen before serving any to your pup.

TIP

Put the peanut butter in a microwave to melt it a little and make it easier to mix.

APPLE CRUNCH CAKES

SWEET TOOTH

1 Preheat the oven to 180°C/350°F/Gas Mark 4.

2 Put 000 ml/20 fl oz of water, 60 ml/ 2 fl oz of apple sauce, 30 ml/1 fl oz of honey, a medium egg and a drop of vanilla extract into a bowl. Mix the ingredients until they are thoroughly combined.

3 Add 250 g/9 oz of wholemeal flour, 100 g/3½ oz of dried apple pieces and 10 g/¼ oz of baking powder. Mix the ingredients until they are thoroughly combined.

4 Put the mixture into the wells of a 12-hole cupcake tin and bake in the oven for 1 hour and 15 minutes. Let the cakes cool before serving any to your pup.

BLUEBERRY BISCUITS

1 Preheat the oven to 190°C/375°F/Gas Mark 5.

2 Wash the blueberries and put them into the blender with the peeled banana and the water. Blend the ingredients together until they form a smooth mixture.

3 Pour the flour and the blueberry mixture into the bowl. Mix the ingredients together to form a dough. Take the dough out of the bowl and put it on to the baking sheet, shaping it with your hands to create a loaf approximately 5 cm/2 inches high.

4 Bake for 20 minutes, or until the top of the loaf feels firm.

5 Take the loaf out of the oven and put it on to the chopping board to cool. Cut the loaf into biscuits that are 1 cm/⅛ inch thick.

6 Place the biscuits on to the baking sheet and put them back into the oven for 20 minutes. Turn each biscuit over and bake for another 20 minutes. Take the biscuits out and leave them to cool.

7 Put the carob chips into the large cup and pour the rapeseed oil on top.

8 Heat in a microwave at full power for 1 minute 20 seconds. Take the cup out of the microwave and mix the melted carob and oil until they are thoroughly combined.

9 Dunk the end of each biscuit into the melted carob and place on to the cool baking sheet. Put the baking sheet in the refrigerator to harden the carob before serving any to your pup.

10 The biscuits can be kept in the refrigerator for four days, or in the freezer for up to one month.

EQUIPMENT

OVEN
SCALES
BLENDER
MEASURING JUG
LARGE MIXING BOWL
MIXING SPOON
BAKING SHEET
CHOPPING BOARD
KNIFE
LARGE MICROWAVEABLE CUP
MICROWAVE

INGREDIENTS

200 G/7 OZ BLUEBERRIES

1 BANANA

225 ML/8 FL OZ WATER

450 G/1 LB PLAIN FLOUR

150 G/5½ OZ CAROB CHIPS

60 ML/2 FL OZ RAPESEED OIL

CHAPTER 5
Allergen-free recipes

SWEET POTATO CRISPS

EQUIPMENT

OVEN
SCALES
CHOPPING BOARD
KNIFE
BAKING SHEET

1 Preheat the oven to 160°C/325°F/Gas Mark 3.

2 Wash the sweet potatoes and put them on to the chopping board. Cut the sweet potatoes into thin slices.

3 Put the sweet potato slices on to the baking sheet and bake them for approximately 30 minutes.

4 Turn the slices over and put them back into the oven for another 30 minutes, or until the slices feel crunchy.

5 Take the slices out of the oven and let them cool before serving any to your pup.

6 The crisps can be kept in the refrigerator for up to seven days, or in the freezer for up to one month.

58

INGREDIENTS

2 LARGE SWEET POTATOES, ABOUT 200 G/7 OZ EACH

PEAR AND BANANA BISCUITS

1 Preheat the oven to 190°C/375°F/Gas Mark 5.

2 Wash the pear and cut it into small pieces. Put the pieces into the blender with the peeled banana and the water.

3 Blend the ingredients together until they form a smooth mixture.

4 Put the pear mixture and the oats into the bowl and mix together until thoroughly combined.

5 Place the oat mixture on a clean surface and roll it out until it is about 1 cm/⅜ inch thick.

6 Cut out as many shapes as you can, depending on the size of your cutter, and place them on the baking sheet.

7 Bake for 30 minutes, or until the biscuits are hard. Let them cool before serving any to your pup.

8 The biscuits can be kept in the refrigerator for up to two weeks.

INGREDIENTS

225 G/8 OZ FRESH PEAR

1 BANANA

225 ML/8 FL OZ WATER

450 G/1 LB GLUTEN-FREE ROLLED OATS

DUCK DELIGHT

1 Preheat the oven to 220°C/425°F/Gas mark 7. Place the duck breast in the baking tray and put it in the oven for 8 minutes.

2 Check that the bottom of the duck breast has browned. Turn the breast over and cook for another 8 minutes. Check that the meat is cooked throughout and the meat is no longer pink.

3 Put the breast on to the chopping board and cut it into cubes about 2.5 cm/1 inch in size.

4 Heat 350 ml/12 fl oz of the water in a saucepan and, once boiling, pour in the rice. Let the rice cook on a low heat for 45 minutes, or until the water is fully absorbed.

5 Peel the carrot and squash, chop the carrot, squash and green beans into small cubes, then add the peas. Put the vegetables and the remaining water into the other saucepan and boil them for 5 minutes.

6 Put the duck, rice and vegetables into the bowl and mix together until thoroughly combined.

7 Allow the mixture to cool to room temperature before serving to your pup.

8 This will make 1-4 servings, depending on the size of your dog. It can also be kept in the refrigerator for two days, or frozen for up to one month.

EQUIPMENT

OVEN
SCALES
BAKING TRAY
CHOPPING BOARD
KNIFE
MEASURING JUG
TWO SAUCEPANS
VEGETABLE PEELER
LARGE MIXING BOWL
MIXING SPOON

INGREDIENTS

1 LARGE DUCK BREAST, ABOUT 225 G/8 OZ

575 ML/18 FL OZ WATER

150 G/5½ OZ RICE

100 G/3½ OZ CARROT

100 G/3½ OZ BUTTERNUT SQUASH

100 G/3½ OZ GREEN BEANS

100 G/3½ OZ PEAS

INDEX

A

allergen-free
  recipes 7,
  56-63
apple 6, 15,
  25, 41
apple sauce 53

B

bacon 18
banana 15, 25,
  44, 52, 54, 60
beef stock 10
biscuits 10-11,
  16-17, 32-33,
  36-37, 38-39,
  48-49, 50-51,
  54-55, 60-61
blueberries 25,
  41, 44, 54
butternut
  squash 28, 62

C

cakes 18-19,
  26-27, 42-43,
  44-45, 52-53
carob chips 6,
  40, 48, 50, 54

carrots 12, 15,
  22, 28, 32,
  34, 62
celery 24
cherries 42
chicken 12
cucumber 22, 28

D

desserts 46-55
dried apple 6,
  53
dried cranberries
  34, 38
duck 62

E

egg 53

F

finding
  ingredients 6
fish stock 16
flour 26, 54
food allergies 7

G

gluten-free
  rolled oats 60
green beans 12,

28, 34, 62

H

harmful foods 7
holiday-themed
  recipes 30-45
honey 18, 36, 53

L

lettuce 22

M

meat recipes
  8-13, 16-19,
  34-35, 62-63

P

Parmesan cheese
  10, 16
peanut butter
  24, 48, 50, 52
pear 15, 60
peas 12, 28,
  34, 62
portion size 6
pumpkin 26

R

rapeseed oil
  40, 48, 50, 54

rice 12, 28,
  34, 62
rolled oats 10,
  16, 18, 32,
  36, 38, 41,
  42, 44, 48

S

storage 7
strawberries
  14, 25, 40
sweet potato
  22, 38, 58

T

turkey 34

V

vanilla extract
  53
vegetarian
  recipes 14-15,
  20-29, 32-33,
  34-45, 48-61

Y

yogurt 22, 52

INDEX

A

allergen-free recipes 7, 56-63

apple 6, 15, 25, 41

apple sauce 53

B

bacon 18

banana 15, 25, 44, 52, 54, 60

beef stock 10

biscuits 10-11, 16-17, 32-33, 36-37, 38-39, 48-49, 50-51, 54-55, 60-61

blueberries 25, 41, 44, 54

butternut squash 28, 62

C

cakes 18-19, 26-27, 42-43, 44-45, 52-53

carob chips 6, 40, 48, 50, 54

carrots 12, 15, 22, 28, 32, 34, 62

celery 24

cherries 42

chicken 12

cucumber 22, 28

D

desserts 46-55

dried apple 6, 53

dried cranberries 34, 38

duck 62

E

egg 53

F

finding ingredients 6

fish stock 16

flour 26, 54

food allergies 7

G

gluten-free rolled oats 60

green beans 12, 28, 34, 62

H

harmful foods 7

holiday-themed recipes 30-45

honey 18, 36, 53

L

lettuce 22

M

meat recipes 8-13, 16-19, 34-35, 62-63

P

Parmesan cheese 10, 16

peanut butter 24, 48, 50, 52

pear 15, 60

peas 12, 28, 34, 62

portion size 6

pumpkin 26

R

rapeseed oil 40, 48, 50, 54

rice 12, 28, 34, 62

rolled oats 10, 16, 18, 32, 36, 38, 41, 42, 44, 48

S

storage 7

strawberries 14, 25, 40

sweet potato 22, 38, 58

T

turkey 34

V

vanilla extract 53

vegetarian recipes 14-15, 20-29, 32-33, 34-45, 48-61

Y

yogurt 22, 52